# Sinful Smoothies

# Sinful Smoothies

## Delicious drinks for everyday indulgence

RYLAND

PETERS

& SMALL

LONDON NEW YORK

First published in 2012 by
Ryland Peters & Small
20–21 Jockey's Fields
London WC1R 4BW
and
519 Broadway, Fifth Floor
New York, NY 10012
www.rylandpeters.com

Text copyright © Louise
Pickford, Tonia George, Ryland
Peters & Small 2012
Design and photographs
© Ryland Peters & Small 2012

10 9 8 7 6 5 4 3 2 1

A CIP record for this book is
available from the British Library.

US Library of Congress
cataloging-in-publication data
has been applied for.

ISBN 978-1-84975-217-6

Printed and bound in China.

**Senior designer**
Toni Kay

**Editor**
Ellen Parnavelas

**Production**
Gary Hayes

**Art director**
Leslie Harrington

**Editorial director**
Julia Charles

# contents

# introduction

Whether it's a fruity morning treat for a lazy Sunday brunch, an ice-blended evening cocktail or a luxurious dessert in a glass, there is sure to be a smoothie here that's perfect for the occasion. Sinful Smoothies is packed full of luscious liquid treats, for an indulgent pick-me-up any time of the day, every day of the week.

With so many creative concoctions to choose from, you'll be surprised how easy it is to elevate the humble smoothie from the realm of healthy treat to one of pure self-indulgence. Forget any idea you may have of smoothies being made just from fruit, juice, yogurt and maybe a splash of milk – there are all kinds of fabulous flavours in this book of delicious beverages.

Tropical Treats like Mango & Ginger Lassi with Yogurt and Pineapple and Passion Fruit Soy Smoothie will transport you to exotic climes. Blissful Berries shows how easy it is to turn delicate berries into something decadent; try Mango & Berry Pash or Iced Berry Blitz. Roll up for Happy Hour and choose from Long Island Milkshake or Passion Fruit Smoothie with Galliano. Serve up a Dreamy Dessert such as Apricot Ice Cream Smoothie or Banana and Peanut Butter Smoothie.

From traditional recipes, such as Blueberry Muesli Smoothie to more original inclusions, such as Chai Vanilla Shake or Peach & Coconut Milk Smoothie, these Sinful Smoothies couldn't be easier or quicker to make, or more enjoyable to consume!

# tropical treats

250 ml/1 cup mango purée, fresh or canned

6 ice cubes

2.5 cm/1 inch piece fresh ginger, peeled and grated

250 ml/1 cup yogurt

sparkling water, ginger ale or reduced fat milk

sugar or honey, to taste (optional)

4 tablespoons diced fresh mango, to serve (optional)

**SERVES 4**

 # mango & ginger lassi with yogurt

Usually, fresh produce is far better than canned. However, if you can find canned Alphonso mango in an Asian market, buy it and try it in this recipe. The Alphonso is famously the greatest mango in the world! Otherwise, use very ripe fresh mango.

Put the mango purée, ice, ginger, yogurt, sparkling water, ginger ale or milk and sugar or honey in a blender or liquidizer and work to a froth. Serve immediately, topped with the diced mango, if using.

# pineapple & ginger smoothie

A delicious fruit smoothie based on the sharbat – the beautiful sweetened fruit drink created for the imperial courts of Muslim rulers from Persia to Moorish Spain, from the Holy Land to Moghul India. This is, of course, the origin of the words 'sherbet' and 'sorbet'.

Working in batches if necessary, put the ginger in a blender or liquidizer, add the pineapple and blend to a smooth purée, adding enough cold water to make the blades run. Taste and add sugar or sugar syrup to taste. Half-fill a jug/pitcher with ice cubes, pour over the pineapple mixture, stir and serve immediately.

Alternatively, add about 10 ice cubes when blending the ginger and pineapple.

2.5 cm/1 inch piece fresh ginger, peeled and grated

1 pineapple, peeled, cored and chopped

sugar or sugar syrup, to taste

ice cubes, to taste

**SERVES 4**

½ pineapple

250 ml/1 cup passion fruit pulp

250 ml/1 cup soy milk

4 scoops vanilla soy ice cream

**SERVES 3**

 # pineapple & passion fruit soy smoothie

Here is a delicious combination of tropical fruit flavours. When choosing a pineapple, pull one of the outside leaves; if ripe, they will pull away easily. The more wrinkled a passion fruit, the riper its flesh. About 8 large passion fruit will yield 250 ml/1 cup of pulp. Canned passion fruit pulp is available from large supermarkets.

Peel the pineapple, discard the tough central core and chop the flesh. Put it in a blender or liquidizer with the passion fruit pulp, soy milk and ice cream. Blend until smooth and serve immediately.

# orange sunset

Reminiscent of the classic cocktail Tequila Sunrise but without the alcohol, this tangy drink is a vibrant orange with a hint of fiery red as the pomegranate juice sinks to the bottom of the glass.

6 oranges

2 pomegranates

**SERVES 2**

Peel the oranges, chop the flesh and press through a juicer into a jug/pitcher. Halve the pomegranates and, using a citrus juicer, squeeze out the juice into a separate jug/pitcher.

Pour the orange juice into 2 tumblers then pour in the pomegranate juice in a thin stream. Serve immediately.

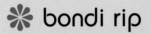 bondi rip

1 large mango,
peeled, stoned
and diced

1 banana, peeled
and sliced

250 ml/1 cup
pineapple juice

50 ml/4  tablespoons
raspberry syrup

ice cubes

**SERVES 2**

Named after Australia's most famous beach,
this is the perfect smoothie for summer. There
are few better ways of watching the world go
by than sipping a glass of this as the heat of
the day fades and the sun worshippers head
home for the night.

Put the mango, banana and pineapple juice
in a blender or liquidizer. Add 6 ice cubes and
whizz until smooth.

To serve, drizzle a little raspberry syrup down the
sides of 2 tall glasses, pour in the blended fruit
and ice mixture and stir well. Serve immediately.

# blissful berries

150 g/1¼ cups raspberries

about 500 ml/2 cups soy milk

12 ice cubes

honey, to taste

**SERVES 4**

 # raspberry smoothie with soy milk

This creamy raspberry smoothie is a perfect non-dairy treat for those who cannot, or prefer not to consume dairy products.

Put the raspberries*, soy milk and ice cubes in a blender and purée to a froth. Serve the honey separately so people can sweeten to taste.

**Note*** If you love raspberries, you can reserve a few and arrange them on top of each glass before serving.

#  blueberry muesli smoothie

This indulgent blueberry smoothie is a delicious morning treat; it is the perfect beverage for a lazy sunday brunch.

Put the blueberries, yogurt, milk and muesli in a blender or liquidizer and purée until smooth. Serve immediately topped with extra blueberries.

250 g/2½ cups fresh or frozen blueberries

250 ml/1 cup yogurt

250 ml/1 cup milk

50 g/½ cup muesli

1 teaspoon pure vanilla extract

a handful of blueberries, to serve

**SERVES 2**

 # iced berry blitz

With all these wonderful frozen berries this is a deliciously refreshing smoothie. The combination of summer fruits makes this the perfect drink for summer.

100 g/³⁄₄ cup frozen raspberries

100 g/³⁄₄ cup frozen strawberries

100 g/³⁄₄ cup frozen blueberries

500 ml/2¹⁄₄ cups apple juice

**SERVES 2**

Put the raspberries, strawberries and blueberries in a blender or liquidizer with the apple juice and blend until smooth. Pour into chilled glasses and serve immediately.

# cherry berry crush

Like a cherry pie in a glass, this cherry smoothie is a rich and delicious treat. It can be topped with grated dark chocolate to make it even more luxurious. If you can't find frozen cherries, use bottled cherries in natural syrup.

Put the cherries, raspberries and sugar in a blender or liquidizer and blend until really smooth.

Pour into chilled glasses and serve immediately topped with grated dark chocolate if desired.

300 g/2¼ cups frozen stoned cherries

125 g/1 cup frozen raspberries

1 tablespoon soft/packed brown sugar

grated dark chocolate, to serve (optional)

**SERVES 2**

100 g/¾ cup
frozen mixed
berries, thawed

1 tablespoon
icing/confectioners'
sugar

1 large mango,
peeled and stoned
(about 250 g/2 cups
flesh)

1 passion fruit, halved

sparkling water,
to top up

ice cubes, to serve

**SERVES 2**

 # mango & berry pash

This classic combination of mango and
berries makes a truly refreshing drink for
a hot summer's day; and with the addition
of the sparkling water it makes a delightful
non-alcoholic cocktail.

Put the berries in a bowl and stir in the icing/
confectioners' sugar, mashing with a fork.
Set aside for 15 minutes, then pass through
a fine-mesh sieve/strainer. Purée the mango
flesh in a blender or liquidizer until smooth
and stir in the passion fruit pulp.

Put a few ice cubes into 2 tall glasses, add
the berry mixture and mango and passion
fruit purée and top up with sparkling water.
Serve immediately.

# happy hour

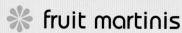 # fruit martinis

250 g/1¼ cups kiwi fruit (4 kiwi fruit)

250 g/1¼ cups strawberries

250 g/2½ cups peeled and cubed watermelon

3 tablespoons caster/superfine sugar

250 ml/1 cup iced vodka

kiwi slices, strawberries and small watermelon wedges, to garnish

ice cubes, lightly crushed, to serve

**SERVES 4–12, AS DESIRED**

**Martinis never tasted or looked so good! Each fruit quantity will make four drinks, so choose whichever flavour you prefer – or why not try one of each?**

Peel and chop the kiwi fruit, hull and halve the strawberries and roughly chop the watermelon.

Purée each fruit separately in a blender or liquidizer with 1 tablespoon sugar, until really smooth. Set aside.

Put each fruit purée separately into a cocktail shaker and add 5 tablespoons iced vodka and a little crushed ice. Replace the lid and shake vigorously for about 30 seconds, remove the lid and pour into 4 martini glasses. Decorate each glass with a slice of fruit and serve immediately.

# long island milkshake

You'll all be familiar with the dangerous cocktail. This milkshake is strictly for adults only – don't be fooled by its innocent name!

Put all the spirits, lemon juice, cola and ice cream in a blender or liquidizer with 2 scoops of crushed ice and whizz until smooth.

Pour into a frosted glass and serve immediately.

15 ml/½ oz. vodka

15 ml/½ oz. gin

15 ml/½ oz. white rum

15 ml/½ oz. tequila

15 ml/½ oz. triple sec

a squeeze of fresh lemon juice

60 ml/¼ cup cola

2 large scoops of vanilla ice cream

crushed ice

**SERVES 1**

 # strawberry liqueur smoothie

250 g/2 cups strawberries, hulled

1 tablespoon strawberry liqueur

3 scoops strawberry ice cream, plus an extra small scoop, to serve

100 ml/scant ½ cup milk, or to taste

**SERVES 1–2**

Old-time American soda jerks were experts at balancing a scoop of ice cream on the edge of the soda glass. If you're not, you could always try balancing yours on a spoon! You can make endless variations of this recipe, matching the liqueur to the fruit – crème de fraise with strawberries, crème de framboise with raspberries, Peach liquer with peaches, and so on.

Place all the ingredients in a blender or liquidizer and whizz. Add extra ice cream for a thicker smoothie, or extra milk, to taste.

Serve in a soda glass with an extra small scoop of ice cream balanced on the edge of the glass (if possible).

# passion fruit smoothie with Galliano

Passion fruit with Galliano liqueur is a terrific combination – and strictly for adults! Verging on a cocktail, this is something to try on a hot summer's afternoon. If you like your smoothie even thicker, add extra ice cream; if you like it smoother, add extra milk, to taste.

Scoop the pulp and seeds of 2 of the passion fruit into a blender or liquidizer, add the Galliano, ice cream and milk, then blend.

Taste, then add sugar and a little extra milk if preferred. Pour the mixture into a glass, top with the remaining passion fruit and serve immediately.

3 passion fruit

1 tablespoon Galliano

3 scoops vanilla ice cream

100 ml/scant ½ cup milk, or to taste

sugar, to taste

**SERVES 1–2**

 ## lemon ice cream soda

80 ml/⅓ cup lemon squash (undiluted)

35 ml/1½ oz. vodka

40 ml/1½ oz. freshly squeezed lemon juice

20 ml/½ oz. sugar syrup

a large scoop of vanilla ice cream

crushed ice

finely pared lemon zest, to garnish

**SERVES 1**

The original 'float' was invented during the late 19th century in the US. In this version, the ingredients are blended together before serving to give it that perfect smooth consistency. You can top with extra scoops of ice cream, if liked.

Put the lemon squash, vodka and juice, sugar syrup and ice cream in a blender or liquidizer.

Add 2 scoops crushed ice and whizz until smooth. Spoon into a chilled martini glass, garnish with a few shreds of lemon zest and serve immediately.

#  cider apple slushie

**While slushies are usually enjoyed by children, this fruity iced treat is definitely one for the grown-ups, and is really worth that little bit of extra effort.**

Put the apple slices, cider, sugar and cinnamon sticks in a saucepan and bring slowly to the boil, stirring until the sugar has dissolved. Cover and simmer gently for 12–15 minutes until the apples are soft.

Remove from the heat and leave to cool. When cool, remove the cinnamon sticks and discard. Transfer the mixture to a blender or liquidizer. Whizz until smooth, then spoon into a freezerproof container and freeze for 4–6 hours.

To serve, return the mixture to the blender and whizz briefly. Pour into tall glasses, garnish with apple slices, if using, and serve immediately.

3 large cooking apples, peeled, cored and sliced

1 litre/4 cups sweet hard cider

250 g/1¼ cups sugar

2 cinnamon sticks, lightly bashed

thinly sliced apple, to garnish (optional)

**SERVES 4**

 ## surf rider

Mix up a creamy Surf Rider and you'll be transported to a Caribbean beach with crystal clear, turquoise waves lapping at the shore. For a tangy treat, try this blended frozen version of a Mojito – it makes a light granita-style ice that's perfect served as a summer dessert.

60 ml/¼ cup Malibu (coconut-flavoured rum)

60 ml/¼ cup fresh pineapple juice

60 ml/¼ cup coconut milk

a small handful of fresh mint leaves

20 ml/½ oz. dark rum

crushed ice

**SERVES 2**

Put the Malibu, pineapple juice, coconut milk and mint in a blender or liquidizer and whizz until smooth.

Spoon the mixture into 2 chilled cocktail glasses and float the dark rum over the top by pouring it in over the back of a spoon. Serve immediately.

# dreamy desserts

2 large, ripe bananas

10 ice cubes

1 tablespoon sugar
or sugar syrup, or
to taste

125 ml/½ cup
milk, yogurt or
single/light cream

4 tablespoons
smooth peanut
butter

**SERVES 1**

# banana & peanut butter smoothie

Bananas make very good smoothies – add them to almost anything else and they will reward you with a sweet creaminess. They have a special affinity with nuts – so the peanut butter here is gorgeous.

Peel and cut the bananas into chunks. Put them in a blender or liquidizer with the ice cubes, sugar, milk, yogurt or cream and peanut butter. Whizz to a purée.

Thin with a little more milk or water if too thick, then serve immediately.

# blueberry ice cream smoothie

This dreamy, creamy smoothie can be made using either vanilla or chocolate ice cream, but blueberries are a particularly good match for chocolate.

Reserve a few blueberries to serve, then put the remainder in a blender or liquidizer. Add the ice cream and enough milk to make the blades run. Blend to a purée, then add extra milk to taste (the less you add, the thicker the smoothie will be).

Pour the mixture into a glass and top with the reserved blueberries and mint leaves, if using. Serve immediately.

1 punnet/basket blueberries, about 200 g/1²⁄₃ cups, chilled

2 scoops ice cream, chocolate or vanilla

about 125 ml/½ cup milk, chilled

fresh mint leaves, to garnish (optional)

**SERVES 1**

 # apricot ice cream smoothie

Apricots, like peaches and nectarines, are too dense to squeeze for juice – you have to purée them in a blender. The ice cream makes the mixture even more indulgent. Leave the skins on and they chop up into little pieces and give a pretty colour and interesting texture.

Put the ice cubes in a blender or liquidizer and blend to a snow. Add the apricot slices, ice cream and apricot nectar. Blend until creamy, adding enough milk or water to make the blades run.

Put the mixture in a glass, swirl in the cream or yogurt, if using, and serve immediately with a spoon.

3 ice cubes

2–3 ripe apricots, halved, stoned and sliced

2 scoops vanilla or strawberry ice cream

1 small carton or can apricot nectar

a little milk or water, as required

2 tablespoons single/light cream or yogurt, to serve (optional)

**SERVES 1**

#  chai vanilla shake

Masala Chai is a traditional beverage from the Indian subcontinent made by brewing tea with a mixture of aromatic spices. This deliciously spiced shake is a chilled variation of this classic Eastern beverage.

Put 800 ml/3 cups of the milk, the sugar, tea leaves, vanilla bean, cinnamon, cardamom and allspice in a saucepan and bring to the boil. Reduce the heat and simmer gently for 5 minutes, then turn off the heat, cover and leave for 10 minutes. Strain into the ice cube trays and freeze until solid.

When ready to serve, put the frozen chai cubes in a blender or liquidizer with the remaining milk and the ice cream and whizz until smooth. Serve immediately.

1 litre/4 cups whole milk

75 g/⅓ cup packed light brown soft sugar

2 tablespoons black tea leaves

1 vanilla bean, split lengthways

¼ teaspoon ground cinnamon

8 cardamom pods

¼ teaspoon ground allspice

3 scoops of vanilla ice cream

ice cube trays

**SERVES 4**

2 bananas

1 teaspoon honey

2 tablespoons
oat bran

2 tablespoons raisins

250 ml/1 cup milk

250 ml/1 cup yogurt

¼ teaspoon freshly
grated nutmeg, plus
extra to dust

**SERVES 2**

# ✳ banana, nutmeg & honey smoothie

This indulgent smoothie is like a banana cream pie in a glass. It can be made with milk, yogurt or cream depending on how indulgent you are feeling. The nutmeg also adds a touch of spice to this delicious treat.

Peel the bananas and chop the flesh. Put them in a blender or liquidizer with the remaining ingredients and blend until smooth. Serve dusted with a little extra grated nutmeg.

# peach & coconut milk smoothie

Although peaches aren't tropical fruits, they work very well with coconut milk in this rich, decadent-tasting smoothie. Other fruit such as apricots, mangoes, bananas or papaya may be used instead of the peaches.

Put the peaches in a blender or liquidizer, add the coconut milk, vanilla, sugar, lime juice and ice cubes and blend until smooth. Taste and add extra sugar if necessary.

Pour into chilled glasses, topped with the shreds of lime zest and serve immediately.

4 large, ripe peaches, peeled, halved, stoned and cut into wedges

250 ml/1 cup canned coconut milk

a few drops of pure vanilla extract

2 tablespoons sugar, or to taste

6 ice cubes

freshly squeezed juice and zest of 1 lime, cut into long shreds

**SERVES 2**

12 ice cubes

4 scoops strawberry ice cream

12 large ripe strawberries, hulled and halved

125 ml/½ cup yogurt

milk

crumbled digestive biscuits/graham crackers to serve (optional)

**SERVES 4**

 # strawberry ice cream smoothie

This delicious smoothie made with strawberry ice cream is the liquid alternative to the strawberry cheesecake. Serve made just with ice, or with yogurt, ice cream or milk. Or (as here) with the lot: self-indulgence is a very good thing!

Put the ice cubes in a blender or liquidizer and blend to a snow. Add the ice cream, strawberries and yogurt and blend again, adding enough milk to give a creamy consistency.

Pour into glasses, top with crumbled digestive biscuits/graham crackers (if using) and serve immediately.

# index

# recipe credits

**Elsa Petersen-Schepelern**

Pages *10, 13, 22, 25, 38, 41, 50, 53, 54, 62*

**Louise Pickford**

Pages *14, 16, 18, 26, 29, 30, 34, 37, 42, 45, 46, 58, 61*

**Tonia George**

Page *57*